I TOTALLY GOT THIS

KNOCK KNOCK®
LOS ANGELES, CALIFORNIA

Created, published, and distributed by Knock Knock
11111 Jefferson Blvd. #5167
Culver City, CA 90231
knockknockstuff.com
Knock Knock is a registered trademark of Knock Knock LLC
Inner-Truth is a registered trademark of Knock Knock LLC

ISBN: 978-168349039-5
UPC: 825703-50154-4

13

I GOT THIS.
I GOT THIS. I GOT THIS.
I DON'T GOT THIS. NOPE. LET'S TRY THAT AGAIN. I TOTALLY GOT THIS! MUCH BETTER.

No matter what you do and how good you are, you're going to doubt yourself sometimes. Everyone has self-doubts. The key to being successful is to take note of these and climb right on over them, reminding yourself that you're hot stuff and you can do whatever you set your mind to. We know, easier said than done.

Sometimes, what you really need to do is fake it. Tell yourself you've got it. Tell everyone else you've got it. In the end, most of the time, you will find that you do indeed "got it." And if you drop it? No big deal. Just say, "I meant to do that!" and pick it back up.

We're not the first to argue that self-confidence will take you far, even when you're not 100 percent certain you have the chops or guts to achieve something. Great thinkers and successful people have been saying this for centuries. The Roman poet Virgil wrote: "They succeed, because they think they can." Samuel Johnson expressed, "Self-confidence is the first requisite to great undertakings." And Theodore Roosevelt asserted it too: "Believe you can and you're halfway there."

Psychologists agree with these great thinkers. *Psychology Today* notes "you can start to build your confidence right now by telling yourself that you've got it in you; the more you believe that you are capable, the more you will be." And if you seem self-assured, if it looks like you believe in yourself, people around you will believe it, too.

So where does this journal come in? As noted self-help guru Deepak Chopra claims, "Journaling is one of the most powerful tools we have to transform our lives." According to a study by James W. Pennebaker and Janel D. Seagal, "Writing about important personal experiences in an emotional way...brings about improvements in mental and physical health." Proven benefits include better stress management, strengthened immune systems, and improvement in chronic illnesses.

It's not entirely clear how journaling accomplishes all this. Catharsis is involved, but many also point to the value of organizing experiences into a cohesive narrative. According to *Newsweek*, some experts believe that journaling "forces us to transform the ruminations cluttering our minds into coherent stories." In many ways, journaling enables us to see beyond doubt and uncertainty so that we can focus on our hopes and aspirations as well as the skills and talents that will take us where we want to go.

Specialists agree that in order to reap the benefits of journaling you have to stick with it, quasi-daily, for as little as five minutes at a time (though at least fifteen minutes is best), even on the days when you're not doubting anything. Finding regular writing times and comfortable locations can help with consistency. If you find yourself unable to rise above "I ain't got it," don't stress. Instead, use the quotes inside this journal as a jumping-off point for observations and explorations.

Write whatever comes, and don't criticize it; journaling is a means of self-reflection, not a structured composition. In other words, spew. Finally, determine a home for your journal where you can find it easily, on days when you've knocked it out of the park and days when couldn't get a single hit. Keep it by your bed, near the fridge, or wherever you keep your sports metaphors.

And you might as well kick off that whole believing in yourself deal this very moment. As actor Hugh Laurie points out, "There's almost no such thing as ready. There's only now. And you may as well do it now. I mean, I say that confidently as if I'm about to go bungee jumping or something—I'm not. I'm not a crazed risk taker. But I do think that, generally speaking, now is as good a time as any." After all, you got this. You really do. Right?

The best motto for a long march is "Don't grumble. Plug on." You hold your future in your own hands.

Sir Frederick Treves

DATE

WHY I SO TOTALLY GOT THIS TODAY:

_____

_____

_____

_____

_____

_____

_____

_____

_____

_____

_____

_____

_____

_____

_____

LEVEL OF CONFIDENCE IN ACTUALLY NAILING IT:

You have brains in your head. You have feet in your shoes. You can steer yourself in any direction you choose.

Dr. Seuss

DATE		

WHY I SO TOTALLY GOT THIS TODAY:

_____

_____

_____

_____

_____

_____

_____

_____

_____

_____

_____

_____

_____

_____

_____

_____

LEVEL OF CONFIDENCE IN ACTUALLY NAILING IT:

**Opportunities
are rarely offered;
they're seized.**

Sheryl Sandberg

	DATE	

WHY I SO TOTALLY GOT THIS TODAY:

_____

_____

_____

_____

_____

_____

_____

_____

_____

_____

_____

_____

_____

_____

_____

_____

_____

LEVEL OF CONFIDENCE IN ACTUALLY NAILING IT:

Without leaps of imagination, or dreaming, we lose the excitement of possibilities. Dreaming, after all, is a form of planning.

Gloria Steinem

WHY I SO TOTALLY GOT THIS TODAY:

_____

_____

_____

_____

_____

_____

_____

_____

_____

_____

_____

_____

_____

_____

_____

_____

LEVEL OF CONFIDENCE IN ACTUALLY NAILING IT:

We work in the dark—
we do what we can—
we give what we have.
Our doubt is our
passion and our
passion is our task.

Henry James

DATE		

WHY I SO TOTALLY GOT THIS TODAY:

_____

_____

_____

_____

_____

_____

_____

_____

_____

_____

_____

_____

_____

_____

_____

_____

LEVEL OF CONFIDENCE IN ACTUALLY NAILING IT:

I know not all that may be coming, but be it what it will, I'll go to it laughing.

Herman Melville

DATE		

WHY I SO TOTALLY GOT THIS TODAY:

_____

_____

_____

_____

_____

_____

_____

_____

_____

_____

_____

_____

_____

_____

_____

_____

LEVEL OF CONFIDENCE IN ACTUALLY NAILING IT:

You can do anything you want in life if you dress for it.

Edith Head

DATE		

WHY I SO TOTALLY GOT THIS TODAY:

_____

_____

_____

_____

_____

_____

_____

_____

_____

_____

_____

_____

_____

_____

_____

LEVEL OF CONFIDENCE IN ACTUALLY NAILING IT:

Life loves
to be taken
by the lapel
and told:
"I'm with
you kid.
Let's go."

Maya Angelou

WHY I SO TOTALLY GOT THIS TODAY:

_____

_____

_____

_____

_____

_____

_____

_____

_____

_____

_____

_____

_____

_____

_____

_____

LEVEL OF CONFIDENCE IN ACTUALLY NAILING IT:

She would be a new person, she vowed. They said no matter how far a mule travels it can never come back a horse, but she would show them all.

Junot Díaz

WHY I SO TOTALLY GOT THIS TODAY:

_____

_____

_____

_____

_____

_____

_____

_____

_____

_____

_____

_____

_____

_____

_____

_____

_____

LEVEL OF CONFIDENCE IN ACTUALLY NAILING IT:

The Sun himself is weak when he first rises, and gathers strength and courage as the day gets on.

Charles Dickens

DATE

WHY I SO TOTALLY GOT THIS TODAY:

_____

_____

_____

_____

_____

_____

_____

_____

_____

_____

_____

_____

_____

_____

_____

_____

_____

_____

LEVEL OF CONFIDENCE IN ACTUALLY NAILING IT:

Where you tend a rose, my lad, a thistle cannot grow.

Frances Hodgson Burnett

WHY I SO TOTALLY GOT THIS TODAY:

_____

_____

_____

_____

_____

_____

_____

_____

_____

_____

_____

_____

_____

_____

_____

_____

_____

_____

LEVEL OF CONFIDENCE IN ACTUALLY NAILING IT:

Don't you worry about me. I'll always come out on top.

Astrid Lindgren

WHY I SO TOTALLY GOT THIS TODAY:

_____

_____

_____

_____

_____

_____

_____

_____

_____

_____

_____

_____

_____

_____

_____

_____

_____

LEVEL OF CONFIDENCE IN ACTUALLY NAILING IT:

Nobody beats Vitas Gerulaitis seventeen times in a row.

Vitas Gerulaitis

WHY I SO TOTALLY GOT THIS TODAY:

_____

_____

_____

_____

_____

_____

_____

_____

_____

_____

_____

_____

_____

_____

_____

_____

LEVEL OF CONFIDENCE IN ACTUALLY NAILING IT:

I know very little about acting. I'm just an incredibly gifted faker.

Robert Downey Jr.

WHY I SO TOTALLY GOT THIS TODAY:

 ·

LEVEL OF CONFIDENCE IN ACTUALLY NAILING IT:

I am the master
of my fate.
I am the captain
of my soul.

William Ernest Henley

WHY I SO TOTALLY GOT THIS TODAY:

_____

_____

_____

_____

_____

_____

_____

_____

_____

_____

_____

_____

_____

_____

_____

_____

LEVEL OF CONFIDENCE IN ACTUALLY NAILING IT:

Sometimes you just have to put on lip gloss and pretend to be psyched.

Mindy Kaling

WHY I SO TOTALLY GOT THIS TODAY:

LEVEL OF CONFIDENCE IN ACTUALLY NAILING IT:

Do. Or do not. There is no try.

Yoda

DATE

WHY I SO TOTALLY GOT THIS TODAY:

_____

_____

_____

_____

_____

_____

_____

_____

_____

_____

_____

_____

_____

_____

_____

_____

LEVEL OF CONFIDENCE IN ACTUALLY NAILING IT:

I have discovered in life that there are ways of getting almost anywhere you want to go, if you *really* want to go.

Langston Hughes

WHY I SO TOTALLY GOT THIS TODAY:

_____

_____

_____

_____

_____

_____

_____

_____

_____

_____

_____

_____

_____

_____

_____

_____

_____

LEVEL OF CONFIDENCE IN ACTUALLY NAILING IT:

If you don't place your foot on the rope, you'll never cross the chasm.

Liz Smith

WHY I SO TOTALLY GOT THIS TODAY:

_____

_____

_____

_____

_____

_____

_____

_____

_____

_____

_____

_____

_____

_____

_____

_____

_____

_____

LEVEL OF CONFIDENCE IN ACTUALLY NAILING IT:

I was amazed that what I needed to survive could be carried on my back. And, most surprising of all, that I could carry it.

Cheryl Strayed

WHY I SO TOTALLY GOT THIS TODAY:

_____

_____

_____

_____

_____

_____

_____

_____

_____

_____

_____

_____

_____

_____

_____

_____

LEVEL OF CONFIDENCE IN ACTUALLY NAILING IT:

You can't be that kid standing at the top of the waterslide, overthinking it. You have to go down the chute.

Tina Fey

WHY I SO TOTALLY GOT THIS TODAY:

_____

_____

_____

_____

_____

_____

_____

_____

_____

_____

_____

_____

_____

_____

LEVEL OF CONFIDENCE IN ACTUALLY NAILING IT:

Don't stop believin' Hold on to the feelin'

Journey

WHY I SO TOTALLY GOT THIS TODAY:

_____

_____

_____

_____

_____

_____

_____

_____

_____

_____

_____

_____

_____

_____

_____

_____

LEVEL OF CONFIDENCE IN ACTUALLY NAILING IT:

You can't connect the dots looking forward; you can only connect them looking backward. So you have to trust that the dots will somehow connect in your future.

Steve Jobs

WHY I SO TOTALLY GOT THIS TODAY:

_____

_____

_____

_____

_____

_____

_____

_____

_____

_____

_____

_____

_____

_____

LEVEL OF CONFIDENCE IN ACTUALLY NAILING IT:

I spoke without fear
of contradiction. I
had done nothing to
prove my position.
But I simply did not
suffer from self-doubt.

Elia Kazan

WHY I SO TOTALLY GOT THIS TODAY:

_____

_____

_____

_____

_____

_____

_____

_____

_____

_____

_____

_____

_____

_____

_____

_____

LEVEL OF CONFIDENCE IN ACTUALLY NAILING IT:

Beware; for I am fearless, and therefore powerful.

Mary Wollstonecraft Shelley

DATE		

WHY I SO TOTALLY GOT THIS TODAY:

_____

_____

_____

_____

_____

_____

_____

_____

_____

_____

_____

_____

_____

_____

_____

LEVEL OF CONFIDENCE IN ACTUALLY NAILING IT:

Let everything happen to you: beauty and terror. Only press on: no feeling is final.

Rainer Maria Rilke

WHY I SO TOTALLY GOT THIS TODAY:

_____

_____

_____

_____

_____

_____

_____

_____

_____

_____

_____

_____

_____

_____

_____

_____

_____

LEVEL OF CONFIDENCE IN ACTUALLY NAILING IT:

All life is an experiment. The more experiments you make, the better. What if they are a little coarse, & you may get your coat soiled or torn? What if you do fail, & get fairly rolled in the dirt once or twice? Up again, you shall never more be so afraid of a tumble.

Ralph Waldo Emerson

WHY I SO TOTALLY GOT THIS TODAY:

_____

_____

_____

_____

_____

_____

_____

_____

_____

_____

_____

_____

_____

_____

_____

LEVEL OF CONFIDENCE IN ACTUALLY NAILING IT:

She must find a boat and sail in it. No guarantee of shore. Only a conviction that what she wanted could exist, if she dared to find it.

Jeanette Winterson

WHY I SO TOTALLY GOT THIS TODAY:

_____

_____

_____

_____

_____

_____

_____

_____

_____

_____

_____

_____

_____

_____

_____

_____

LEVEL OF CONFIDENCE IN ACTUALLY NAILING IT:

When we
own our
stories, we
get to write
the ending.

Brené Brown

WHY I SO TOTALLY GOT THIS TODAY:

_____

_____

_____

_____

_____

_____

_____

_____

_____

_____

_____

_____

_____

_____

_____

_____

LEVEL OF CONFIDENCE IN ACTUALLY NAILING IT:

We are the ones we've been waiting for. We are the change that we seek.

Barack Obama

DATE

WHY I SO TOTALLY GOT THIS TODAY:

_____

_____

_____

_____

_____

_____

_____

_____

_____

_____

_____

_____

_____

_____

_____

_____

_____

LEVEL OF CONFIDENCE IN ACTUALLY NAILING IT:

This is the fast lane, folks...and some of us like it here.

Hunter S. Thompson

DATE		

WHY I SO TOTALLY GOT THIS TODAY:

_____

_____

_____

_____

_____

_____

_____

_____

_____

_____

_____

_____

_____

_____

_____

LEVEL OF CONFIDENCE IN ACTUALLY NAILING IT:

Life is always a tightrope or a feather bed. Give me the tightrope.

Edith Wharton

WHY I SO TOTALLY GOT THIS TODAY:

_____

_____

_____

_____

_____

_____

_____

_____

_____

_____

_____

_____

_____

_____

_____

_____

_____

LEVEL OF CONFIDENCE IN ACTUALLY NAILING IT:

No matter what happens,
if I get pushed down,
I'm going to come right
back up.

Doris Day

WHY I SO TOTALLY GOT THIS TODAY:

_____

_____

_____

_____

_____

_____

_____

_____

_____

_____

_____

_____

_____

_____

_____

LEVEL OF CONFIDENCE IN ACTUALLY NAILING IT:

My passions were all gathered together like fingers that made a fist.

Bette Davis

DATE		

WHY I SO TOTALLY GOT THIS TODAY:

_____

_____

_____

_____

_____

_____

_____

_____

_____

_____

_____

_____

_____

_____

_____

_____

LEVEL OF CONFIDENCE IN ACTUALLY NAILING IT:

A quilt may take a year, but if you just keep doing it, you get a quilt.

Chuck Close

WHY I SO TOTALLY GOT THIS TODAY:

_____

_____

_____

_____

_____

_____

_____

_____

_____

_____

_____

_____

_____

_____

_____

_____

LEVEL OF CONFIDENCE IN ACTUALLY NAILING IT:

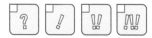

Perseverance is a great element
of success. If you only knock long
enough and loud enough at the gate,
you are sure to wake up somebody.

Henry Wadsworth Longfellow

WHY I SO TOTALLY GOT THIS TODAY:

_____

_____

_____

_____

_____

_____

_____

_____

_____

_____

_____

_____

_____

_____

_____

_____

LEVEL OF CONFIDENCE IN ACTUALLY NAILING IT:

Who climbs with toil, wheresoe'er,
Shall find wings waiting there.

Henry Charles Beeching

WHY I SO TOTALLY GOT THIS TODAY:

_____

_____

_____

_____

_____

_____

_____

_____

_____

_____

_____

_____

_____

_____

_____

_____

LEVEL OF CONFIDENCE IN ACTUALLY NAILING IT:

A dame that knows the ropes isn't likely to get tied up.

Mae West

WHY I SO TOTALLY GOT THIS TODAY:

LEVEL OF CONFIDENCE IN ACTUALLY NAILING IT:

The one thing that you have that nobody else has is *you*. Your voice, your mind, your story, your vision. So write and draw and build and play and dance and live as only you can.

Neil Gaiman

WHY I SO TOTALLY GOT THIS TODAY:

_____

_____

_____

_____

_____

_____

_____

_____

_____

_____

_____

_____

_____

_____

_____

LEVEL OF CONFIDENCE IN ACTUALLY NAILING IT:

Tough times never last, but tough people do!

Robert H. Schuller

DATE		

WHY I SO TOTALLY GOT THIS TODAY:

_____

_____

_____

_____

_____

_____

_____

_____

_____

_____

_____

_____

_____

_____

_____

_____

LEVEL OF CONFIDENCE IN ACTUALLY NAILING IT:

Vitality shows in not only the ability to persist but the ability to start over.

F. Scott Fitzgerald

WHY I SO TOTALLY GOT THIS TODAY:

_____

_____

_____

_____

_____

_____

_____

_____

_____

_____

_____

_____

_____

LEVEL OF CONFIDENCE IN ACTUALLY NAILING IT:

Woe-is-me is not an attractive narrative.

Maureen Dowd

DATE		

WHY I SO TOTALLY GOT THIS TODAY:

_____

_____

_____

_____

_____

_____

_____

_____

_____

_____

_____

_____

_____

_____

_____

_____

_____

LEVEL OF CONFIDENCE IN ACTUALLY NAILING IT:

What seem to us bitter trials
are often blessings in disguise.

Oscar Wilde

WHY I SO TOTALLY GOT THIS TODAY:

LEVEL OF CONFIDENCE IN ACTUALLY NAILING IT:

It is a common experience that a problem difficult at night is resolved in the morning after the committee of sleep has worked on it.

John Steinbeck

WHY I SO TOTALLY GOT THIS TODAY:

_____

_____

_____

_____

_____

_____

_____

_____

_____

_____

_____

_____

_____

_____

_____

_____

_____

LEVEL OF CONFIDENCE IN ACTUALLY NAILING IT:

I like breakfast-time better than
any other moment in the day....
No dust has settled on one's mind
then, and it presents a clear mirror
to the rays of things.

George Eliot

WHY I SO TOTALLY GOT THIS TODAY:

LEVEL OF CONFIDENCE IN ACTUALLY NAILING IT:

It is the same with people as it is with riding a bike. Only when moving can one comfortably maintain one's balance.

Albert Einstein

WHY I SO TOTALLY GOT THIS TODAY:

LEVEL OF CONFIDENCE IN ACTUALLY NAILING IT:

I feel pretty
Oh, so pretty
That the city should
  give me its key.
A committee
should be organized
  to honor me.

Stephen Sondheim

DATE		

WHY I SO TOTALLY GOT THIS TODAY:

_____

_____

_____

_____

_____

_____

_____

_____

_____

_____

_____

_____

_____

_____

_____

_____

_____

LEVEL OF CONFIDENCE IN ACTUALLY NAILING IT:

Fearlessness is not the absence of fear. Rather, it's the mastery of fear.

Arianna Huffington

DATE		

WHY I SO TOTALLY GOT THIS TODAY:

_____

_____

_____

_____

_____

_____

_____

_____

_____

_____

_____

_____

_____

_____

_____

_____

LEVEL OF CONFIDENCE IN ACTUALLY NAILING IT:

It's okay
is a cosmic
truth.

Richard Bach

WHY I SO TOTALLY GOT THIS TODAY:

_____

_____

_____

_____

_____

_____

_____

_____

_____

_____

_____

_____

_____

_____

_____

_____

_____

LEVEL OF CONFIDENCE IN ACTUALLY NAILING IT:

As you get older, you're not afraid of doubt. Doubt isn't running the show. You take out all the self-agonizing.

Clint Eastwood

DATE		

WHY I SO TOTALLY GOT THIS TODAY:

_____

_____

_____

_____

_____

_____

_____

_____

_____

_____

_____

_____

_____

_____

_____

_____

LEVEL OF CONFIDENCE IN ACTUALLY NAILING IT:

Talent is luck. The important thing in life is courage.

Woody Allen

WHY I SO TOTALLY GOT THIS TODAY:

_____

_____

_____

_____

_____

_____

_____

_____

_____

_____

_____

_____

_____

_____

_____

LEVEL OF CONFIDENCE IN ACTUALLY NAILING IT:

I can't think of anyone I admire
who isn't fueled by self-doubt.
It's an essential ingredient.
It's the grit in the oyster.

Richard Eyre

WHY I SO TOTALLY GOT THIS TODAY:

_____

_____

_____

_____

_____

_____

_____

_____

_____

_____

_____

_____

_____

_____

_____

_____

_____

LEVEL OF CONFIDENCE IN ACTUALLY NAILING IT:

A career is built one paragraph at a time.

Barbara Kingsolver

WHY I SO TOTALLY GOT THIS TODAY:

_____

_____

_____

_____

_____

_____

_____

_____

_____

_____

_____

_____

_____

_____

_____

_____

LEVEL OF CONFIDENCE IN ACTUALLY NAILING IT:

Ever tried. Ever failed.
No matter. Try again.
Fail again. Fail better.

Samuel Beckett

WHY I SO TOTALLY GOT THIS TODAY:

_____

_____

_____

_____

_____

_____

_____

_____

_____

_____

_____

_____

_____

_____

_____

_____

LEVEL OF CONFIDENCE IN ACTUALLY NAILING IT:

I am so smart. I am so smart.
I am so smart. I am so smart.
S-M-R-T—I mean S-M-A-R-T.

Homer Simpson

WHY I SO TOTALLY GOT THIS TODAY:

_____

_____

_____

_____

_____

_____

_____

_____

_____

_____

_____

_____

_____

_____

_____

_____

_____

LEVEL OF CONFIDENCE IN ACTUALLY NAILING IT:

I was someone with not much self-belief at all and yet in this one thing in my life I believed. That was the one thing in my life. I felt "I can tell a story."

J. K. Rowling

WHY I SO TOTALLY GOT THIS TODAY:

_____

_____

_____

_____

_____

_____

_____

_____

_____

_____

_____

_____

_____

_____

_____

LEVEL OF CONFIDENCE IN ACTUALLY NAILING IT:

There's not a thing wrong with you, you're right all the way through.

Emma Donoghue

WHY I SO TOTALLY GOT THIS TODAY:

_____

_____

_____

_____

_____

_____

_____

_____

_____

_____

_____

_____

_____

_____

_____

_____

_____

LEVEL OF CONFIDENCE IN ACTUALLY NAILING IT:

I am a champion
and you're gonna
hear me roar.

Katy Perry

WHY I SO TOTALLY GOT THIS TODAY:

_____

_____

_____

_____

_____

_____

_____

_____

_____

_____

_____

_____

_____

_____

_____

_____

LEVEL OF CONFIDENCE IN ACTUALLY NAILING IT:

When all else fails,
you always have delusion.

Conan O'Brien

DATE

WHY I SO TOTALLY GOT THIS TODAY:

_____

_____

_____

_____

_____

_____

_____

_____

_____

_____

_____

_____

_____

_____

_____

LEVEL OF CONFIDENCE IN ACTUALLY NAILING IT:

Let other pens dwell on guilt and misery.

Jane Austen

WHY I SO TOTALLY GOT THIS TODAY:

_____

_____

_____

_____

_____

_____

_____

_____

_____

_____

_____

_____

_____

_____

_____

_____

_____

LEVEL OF CONFIDENCE IN ACTUALLY NAILING IT:

God knows, there's enough to worry about without worrying about worrying about things.

Edward Gorey

WHY I SO TOTALLY GOT THIS TODAY:

_____

_____

_____

_____

_____

_____

_____

_____

_____

_____

_____

_____

_____

_____

_____

LEVEL OF CONFIDENCE IN ACTUALLY NAILING IT:

Leave it to me: I'm always top banana in the shock department.

Truman Capote

WHY I SO TOTALLY GOT THIS TODAY:

LEVEL OF CONFIDENCE IN ACTUALLY NAILING IT:

Every day is a new beginning and a chance to blow it.

Cathy Guisewite

WHY I SO TOTALLY GOT THIS TODAY:

_____

_____

_____

_____

_____

_____

_____

_____

_____

_____

_____

_____

_____

_____

_____

_____

_____

LEVEL OF CONFIDENCE IN ACTUALLY NAILING IT:

And the trouble is, if you don't risk anything, you risk even *more*.

Erica Jong

DATE		

WHY I SO TOTALLY GOT THIS TODAY:

_____

_____

_____

_____

_____

_____

_____

_____

_____

_____

_____

_____

_____

_____

_____

_____

LEVEL OF CONFIDENCE IN ACTUALLY NAILING IT:

It's a good thing to have all the props pulled out from under us occasionally. It gives us some sense of what is rock under our feet, and what is sand.

Madeleine L'Engle

DATE		

WHY I SO TOTALLY GOT THIS TODAY:

_____

_____

_____

_____

_____

_____

_____

_____

_____

_____

_____

_____

_____

_____

_____

_____

_____

LEVEL OF CONFIDENCE IN ACTUALLY NAILING IT:

Courage is being scared
to death—and saddling
up anyway.

John Wayne

WHY I SO TOTALLY GOT THIS TODAY:

_____

_____

_____

_____

_____

_____

_____

_____

_____

_____

_____

_____

_____

_____

LEVEL OF CONFIDENCE IN ACTUALLY NAILING IT:

Life is either a daring adventure or nothing.

Helen Keller

DATE

WHY I SO TOTALLY GOT THIS TODAY:

_____

_____

_____

_____

_____

_____

_____

_____

_____

_____

_____

_____

_____

_____

_____

LEVEL OF CONFIDENCE IN ACTUALLY NAILING IT:

Failure isn't the enemy—fear is.
One learns, after all, by failing.
This is elementary; we all know it,
except when it applies to ourselves.

Carla Needleman

WHY I SO TOTALLY GOT THIS TODAY:

_____

_____

_____

_____

_____

_____

_____

_____

_____

_____

_____

_____

_____

_____

_____

LEVEL OF CONFIDENCE IN ACTUALLY NAILING IT:

Make it work.

Tim Gunn

WHY I SO TOTALLY GOT THIS TODAY:

_____

_____

_____

_____

_____

_____

_____

_____

_____

_____

_____

_____

_____

_____

_____

LEVEL OF CONFIDENCE IN ACTUALLY NAILING IT:

When asked, "How do you write?" I invariably answer, "One word at a time."

Stephen King

WHY I SO TOTALLY GOT THIS TODAY:

_____

_____

_____

_____

_____

_____

_____

_____

_____

_____

_____

_____

_____

_____

_____

LEVEL OF CONFIDENCE IN ACTUALLY NAILING IT:

Be strong, be brave, be true. Endure.

Dave Eggers

WHY I SO TOTALLY GOT THIS TODAY:

_____

_____

_____

_____

_____

_____

_____

_____

_____

_____

_____

_____

_____

_____

_____

_____

_____

_____

LEVEL OF CONFIDENCE IN ACTUALLY NAILING IT:

If you have the guts
to be yourself...other
people'll pay your price.

John Updike

WHY I SO TOTALLY GOT THIS TODAY:

_____

_____

_____

_____

_____

_____

_____

_____

_____

_____

_____

_____

_____

_____

_____

LEVEL OF CONFIDENCE IN ACTUALLY NAILING IT:

You need to learn how to select your thoughts just the same way you select what clothes you're gonna wear every day. This is a power you can cultivate.

Elizabeth Gilbert

WHY I SO TOTALLY GOT THIS TODAY:

_____

_____

_____

_____

_____

_____

_____

_____

_____

_____

_____

_____

_____

_____

_____

LEVEL OF CONFIDENCE IN ACTUALLY NAILING IT:

The world is a wheel,
and it will all come
round right.

Benjamin Disraeli

DATE		

WHY I SO TOTALLY GOT THIS TODAY:

LEVEL OF CONFIDENCE IN ACTUALLY NAILING IT:

I think there should be
a rule that everyone in
the world should get a
standing ovation at least
once in their lives.

R. J. Palacio

WHY I SO TOTALLY GOT THIS TODAY:

_____

_____

_____

_____

_____

_____

_____

_____

_____

_____

_____

_____

_____

_____

_____

_____

LEVEL OF CONFIDENCE IN ACTUALLY NAILING IT:

Bunkum and tummyrot!
You'll never get anywhere
if you go about what-iffing
like that.... We want no
whatiffers around here.

Roald Dahl

DATE

WHY I SO TOTALLY GOT THIS TODAY:

_____

_____

_____

_____

_____

_____

_____

_____

_____

_____

_____

_____

_____

_____

_____

LEVEL OF CONFIDENCE IN ACTUALLY NAILING IT:

Trust yourself. You know more than you think you do.

Dr. Benjamin Spock

WHY I SO TOTALLY GOT THIS TODAY:

_____

_____

_____

_____

_____

_____

_____

_____

_____

_____

_____

_____

_____

_____

_____

_____

LEVEL OF CONFIDENCE IN ACTUALLY NAILING IT:

Yup. Nailed it.

Knock Knock